The Perfect Cat Owner's Guide

Mastering the Art of Feline Care and Companionship

Janice V Garrett, DVM

ISBN: 978-1-989849-14-9

DEDICATION

For all the cats in the world
and the humans who love them.

TABLE OF CONTENTS

DEDICATION 3

TABLE OF CONTENTS 5

ACKNOWLEDGMENTS 6

CHAPTER 1 INTRODUCTION 7

CHAPTER 2 Decoding Feline
Communication 13

CHAPTER 3 Environmental Enrichment .. 17

CHAPTER 4 Catering to Kitty: The
A to Z of Cat Nutrition and Diet 23

CHAPTER 5 Purrfect Playtime: Building
a Strong Bond through Play and Exercise.. 33

CHAPTER 6 Navigating Health and
Wellness: Preventing and Managing
Common Feline Health Issues 41

CHAPTER 7 Feline Socialization:
Building Strong Relationships with
Other Cats and Humans 51

CHAPTER 8 Safety First 59

CHAPTER 9 Traveling with Your Cat:
Tips for a Safer Trip 69

CHAPTER 10 Senior Cat Care: Tips for
Supporting Your Aging Feline Friend 73

ABOUT THE AUTHOR 79

ACKNOWLEDGMENTS

Many thanks to all the cats and the people I have worked with and loved for many years as a feline practitioner in a veterinary practice devoted to cats.

To Edward B. Leeds, DVM, thank you for all your help and guidance early in my veterinary career.

CHAPTER 1
INTRODUCTION

Cats can bring joy, companionship, and a unique sense of humor to our lives, often enriching our days in ways we could never have imagined. However, being a cat owner also comes with its share of responsibilities. In this chapter, we will explore the importance of responsible cat ownership, the role of a perfect cat owner, and set the foundation for building a solid human-cat bond.

The Importance of Responsible Cat Ownership/Guardianship/ Parenting

If you have adopted a cat, you significantly impact your feline friend's health, happiness, and overall quality of life. Cats depend on us for their basic needs, such as food, shelter, medical care, and companionship. Responsible cat parenting involves meeting these essential needs and going above and beyond to create a nurturing, stimulating, and loving environment where your cat can thrive.

A responsible cat person also extends beyond the walls of your home. As a cat parent, you must ensure your pet does not negatively impact the environment or other animals. This includes practicing responsible pet population control through spaying or neutering and keeping your cat safely contained indoors or in a secure outdoor enclosure. In doing so, you protect your cat from potential dangers and contribute to the well-being of your community and the environment.

The Role of a Perfect Cat Person

Let's talk about this book and its title. I loved the cover image of a cat reading a guide about humans. The reality is that cats are a mystery never to be solved. They understand things we don't understand, they sense things we don't sense, and these abilities and perceptions are part of their gifts to us and the world.

Being a perfect cat person is not about striving for an unattainable ideal but rather about embracing a mindset that prioritizes your cat's well-being and constantly seeks to deepen your understanding of your feline companion. A perfect cat owner is one who:

Listens and observes: Takes the time to understand their cat's unique personality, preferences, and communication style.

Educates themselves: Continually learn about feline behavior, health, and care to provide their cat the best possible environment and support.

Practices patience and empathy: Recognizes that cats, like humans, have their quirks, challenges, and needs and approaches these with patience, understanding, and a willingness to adapt.

Makes informed decisions: Considers the short and long-term impacts of their choices on their cat's health, happiness, and well-being and makes decisions accordingly.

Prioritizes their cat's needs: Consistently put their physical, emotional, and social needs at the forefront as best as possible.

Setting the Foundation for a Strong Human-Cat Bond

Building a strong bond with your cat is the heart of being a perfect cat owner. Based on trust, understanding, and mutual respect, this bond enhances your relationship with your cat and contributes to their and your overall health and happiness. Here are some fundamental principles to consider as you begin your journey as a cat owner:

Start on the right foot: Whether you're adopting a kitten or an adult cat, the initial days and weeks in their new home are crucial for establishing a solid foundation for your relationship. First, create a safe, quiet space for your cat to explore and settle in, and allow them to approach you at their own pace. This will help build trust and a sense of security.

Pay attention to your cat's body language, vocalizations, and other forms of communication.

Providing for your cat's basic needs for food, water, shelter, and affection can help build trust and connection. Some cats adore being petted, and others not so much.

Engage in interactive play: Play is a vital component of your cat's physical and mental well-being and an excellent way to strengthen your bond. Schedule regular play sessions using toys that encourage your cat's natural hunting instincts, such as wand toys or puzzle feeders. This shared activity provides mental and physical stimulation and allows you to understand your cat's preferences and behaviors better.

Offer positive reinforcement: Reward your cat with praise, treats, or affection when they exhibit desirable behaviors. Avoid punishment, as it can damage your bond and create fear or anxiety in your cat.

Respect your cat's boundaries: Like humans, cats have individual boundaries and personal space requirements. Please pay attention to your cat's body language and respect their limits.

Be patient and adaptable: Building a strong bond with your cat can take time and patience. Remember that each cat is different, and it may take longer to establish a deep connection with some cats than others.

In the following chapters, we will delve deeper into specific aspects of cat care and companionship, providing practical tips, insights, and strategies to help you become your cat's best guardian, friend, and companion.

CHAPTER 2
Decoding Feline Communication

Cracking the Cat Code

Ever wondered what your cat is trying to tell you when they suddenly burst into an impassioned aria of meows? Or when they perform their best Halloween cat impression with a puffed-up tail?

Understanding Cat Body Language

A cat's body language provides us with clues to their emotions and intentions. Here are some key body language cues to look out for:

Relaxed posture: A friendly and relaxed cat will walk with their tail held high.

Defensive posture: A defensive cat may arch their back and puff their fur while hissing or growling. It's best to give them some space.

Offensive posture: A cat with ears flattened against their head. Give them room to cool down.

The Opera of Cat Vocalizations

Purring: Like a tiny, furry engine of happiness, purring usually means your cat is content. But beware, it can also mean they're in pain, so always pay attention to context.

Meowing: Cats primarily meow to communicate their desires.

Chirping or chattering: This is a cat's sound, usually when observing birds or other prey (bugs and such).

Hissing or growling: The feline version of "Watch Out." This is your cat's way of telling everyone to back off.

Facial Expressions and Tail Signals: The Art of Feline Interpretive Dance

Cats use their faces and tails to express themselves.

Eyes: Dilated pupils can mean fear. Narrow pupils can indicate aggression. Slow blinking, on the other hand, is usually a calm kitty. If looking at them, slow blinking may help calm them.

Whiskers: Whiskers are a cat's facial accessories that serve a purpose. Cats use their whiskers to detect the size of holes. So if they are on a mouse hunt, they won't get their head trapped in a mouse hole, sensing the size first with their whiskers. It is best to use an open flat plate for food, and for drinking, use a bowl filled close to the top or even a fountain to keep their whiskers from touching the sides of the bowl. Is your cat hesitant to eat or drink? Ask yourself if the bowl may be too deep and the whiskers are touching the sides.

Ears: A cat's ears are like little satellite dishes that help them pick up sounds. Ears forward mean on alert. Ears flattened might mean fear or aggression.

Paws: Some call it kneading. Some call it making kitty biscuits. They are using their feet as if they were making bread. It is often combined with purring and maybe some sucking as they did as a kitten nursing on their mother. Most cat people love to see their cats this content. Unfortunately, these cats may have been weaned too soon from their mothers. To protect your skin from the sharp kitty nails of an overly enthusiastic kneading kitty, grab a towel or blanket to put on your lap first before the kneading begins.

CHAPTER 3
Environmental Enrichment

Cats can be notoriously independent, and just like us, our feline friends need an environment that caters to their needs, preferences, and quirky personalities. In this chapter, we'll explore how to create a place.

A cardboard box may do the trick for some. Some love an empty paper sack from the grocery store. Trim off the bag's handle to prevent their head from getting caught in the handle by accident.

Safe spaces: Every cat dreams of a cozy nook to retreat from the stresses of their hectic, nap-filled lives. Provide your cat multiple hide-holes, like covered beds, boxes, or strategically placed blankets.

Vertical space: Cats are natural-born climbers with a penchant for perching on high places. Cat trees, shelves, or window perches are fun for most cats.

Scratching surfaces: Cats need to scratch for good nail care. To save your furniture and sanity, offer various scratching options, such as posts, pads, and cardboard scratchers.

Feeding stations: Set up feeding stations in quiet, low-traffic areas. Cats love running water. Consider getting a fountain...be sure to change the water daily if using a bowl. Bowls and dishes should be made of glass, stainless steel, ceramic, or paper, not plastic. Some cats are thought to develop feline acne on their chins, which may be triggered or aggravated by plastic bowls and dishes. Why? Plastic may retain bacteria, or is it a primary reaction to the plastic itself? Do not place their food and water bowls next to their litter box. It may be too smelly for them, even if it looks clean.

Litter box: Your cat's bathroom should be clean and free of artificial fragrances. Place litter boxes in private, easily accessible locations and clean them regularly. If possible, do not place the litter box near the washer and dryer or other noisy areas. For example, the tennis shoes in the dryer knocking around can deter a cat from using the box. How many cat litter pans? Some say at least one per cat, plus one placed in a different location.

The Art of Enrichment: Building a Cat Wonderland

A stimulating environment is essential for your cat's physical and mental well-being. Here are some tips to keep your cat entertained and engaged:

New toys: Some cats have short attention spans and may tire of a toy. Set it aside and offer it again another day. On the other hand, some cats appreciate new toys or have a special toy or choose one of your stuffed animals as their favorite. My cat, Taffy, liked to play catch when she was on her cat tree. I would toss her a tiny fluffy toy, and she would catch it with one paw.

Puzzle feeders: Some cats like the challenge of puzzle feeders or treat-dispensing toys.

DIY enrichment: Get creative with DIY cat toys and games. A crumpled-up ball of paper, an empty cardboard box, or a paper bag can become your cat's new favorite plaything.

Schedule playtime: Daily play sessions to keep your cat physically active, mentally stimulated, and, maybe, tired enough not to wake you up at 3 am demanding attention.

Access to the outdoors: Create a secure screened-in enclosure in your yard.

Environmental Harmony: Integrating Feline and Human Spaces

Creating a cat-friendly environment doesn't mean sacrificing your sense of style and comfort. Here are some tips for integrating feline and human spaces:

Choose pet-friendly furniture: Opt for furniture made of durable, easy-to-clean materials that can withstand the occasional clawing or hairball incident. Consider choosing fabrics and colors that match your cat's fur to camouflage shedding.

Keep breakables out of reach: Display fragile items in closed cabinets or high shelves out of pouncing range.

Embrace a stylish cat tree: Gone are the days when cat trees and scratching posts were limited to a few choices.

Maintain cleanliness: Keep the litter box clean: Regularly clean the litter boxes decreasing any potential odor concerns. I scoop at least once or twice daily and weekly, dump all the litter, and wash the pan with soapy water. Don't use scented or strong-smelling cleaners. Strong odors can deter the use of the litter box by the cat. They may choose a rug instead of the litter box if the litter box is aversive to them. Many cats prefer uncovered litter boxes even though many humans prefer them covered. We want them to use the litter pan rather than other places in the house.

In conclusion, create a living space that will work for you and your cat. You can create a wonderful home for both of you with creativity, planning, and attention to detail.

CHAPTER 4
Catering to Kitty: The A to Z of Cat Nutrition and Diet

Welcome to the Feline Culinary Academy

Cats are notorious for being picky eaters, but as a perfect cat parent, you must ensure your feline friend receives the nutrition they need to live their best nine lives. In this chapter, we'll explore the culinary world of cat nutrition, from deciphering food labels to understanding your cat's dietary requirements. So, grab your apron and chef's hat – we're about to get cooking!

The Science of Cat Nutrition:

Building Blocks for a Healthy Feline

Cats are obligate carnivores, requiring a diet rich in animal-based proteins to thrive. Understanding the components of a balanced cat diet will help you make informed choices about what to feed your feline friend:

1. Protein: As natural-born hunters, cats need a high-protein diet to support their growth, maintenance, and overall health. Animal-based proteins are essential, as they contain the full range of amino acids cats require, including taurine, which is crucial for heart health and vision. Do not feed your cat dog food. Dog food is not nutritionally complete enough for your cat.

2. Fats: Fat is a vital source of energy for cats and helps them absorb essential fat-soluble vitamins. Healthy fat sources include fish oil and animal fat, which provide essential fatty acids, like omega-3 and omega-6, for healthy skin, coat, and immune system function.

3. Vitamins and minerals: Cats need a range of vitamins and minerals for optimal health, like calcium and phosphorus for strong bones and teeth, and B vitamins for healthy brain function. High-quality cat food should provide all the necessary nutrients in the right balance.

4. Carbohydrates: While cats don't have a strict dietary requirement for carbohydrates, they can be a source of energy and fiber. However, avoiding excessive carbohydrate intake is essential, as it can contribute to obesity and other health issues.

5. Water: Hydration is crucial for your cat's health, so always provide fresh water. Wet food can also be a valuable source of moisture, especially for cats who are reluctant drinkers.

Decoding Cat Food Labels: A Crash Course in Feline Fine Dining

Navigating the world of cat food can be a daunting task. Here's how to decode food labels and make the best choices for your feline companion:

1. Check the ingredients: Look for high-quality, named animal protein sources as the first ingredient, such as chicken, turkey, or salmon. Avoid unspecified meat by-products and fillers like corn, wheat, and soy.

2. Assess the nutritional content: Review the Guaranteed Analysis panel on the label to ensure the food meets your cat's dietary requirements. Look for high protein, moderate fat, and minimal carbohydrates.

3. Look for AAFCO statements: The Association of American Feed Control Officials (AAFCO) sets guidelines for pet food nutrition. Look for a statement indicating the food is formulated to meet AAFCO nutrient profiles or has undergone feeding trials to ensure it's nutritionally complete.

4. Consider life stage and dietary needs: Choose cat food tailored to your cat's life stage (kitten, adult, or senior) and specific nutritional requirements, such as weight management or hairball control.

5. Monitor recalls and reviews: Research the cat food brand's history and reputation, including any recalls or safety issues. Reading reviews from fellow cat owners can also provide valuable insight into the quality and palatability of the food.

Dry vs. Wet Food: The Great Cat Food Debate

Choosing between dry and wet cat food can be a contentious topic among cat owners. However, there are certain conditions where wet food is needed, and I recommend an early introduction. I feed primarily canned food and maybe some dry.

Both types of food have advantages and disadvantages, so weighing your options and considering your cat's specific needs and preferences is essential.

1. Dry food: Dry kibble is convenient, less expensive, and has a longer shelf life than wet food. It might help reduce plaque buildup on your cat's teeth. Dry food is low in moisture, so it's essential to ensure your cat drinks enough water to stay hydrated. I don't recommend adding water to kibble. Instead, supply fresh water in a separate bowl or fountain. I recommend tossing uneaten dry kibble in a bowl and cleaning the bowls regularly. The old kibble at the bottom of the bowl can get moldy and stale.

2. Wet food: Wet or canned cat food provides additional moisture, which can be particularly beneficial for cats prone to urinary tract issues or those not drinking enough water. Wet food can be more expensive and spoil quickly once opened, but many cats find it more palatable than dry kibble. Slightly heated canned food below body temperature is the most palatable for most cats.

Feeding Guidelines: How Much and How Often?

Determining the right amount and frequency of feeding for your cat is crucial for maintaining a healthy weight and avoiding overeating. Here are some guidelines to help you navigate the world of cat portion control:

1. Read the label: Most cat food packages provide feeding guidelines based on your cat's weight and life stage. These recommendations can be a useful starting point, but adjusting the portions according to your cat's specific needs and activity level is essential.

2. Monitor weight and body condition: Regularly weigh your cat and assess their body condition to ensure they maintain a healthy weight. Adjust food portions and feeding frequency accordingly. Dry kibble is the most calorie dense.

3. Consider meal frequency: Cats are natural grazers and may prefer to eat

small, frequent meals throughout the day. Some owners free-feed dry kibble, allowing their cats to graze at their leisure, while others prefer to offer scheduled meals to prevent overeating.

4. Consult your veterinarian: Your vet can provide personalized recommendations on the appropriate type, amount, and feeding frequency for your cat based on age, weight, health, and lifestyle.

Treats and Extras: Indulging Your Cat Responsibly

Treats can be a fun way to bond with your cat and reward good behavior, but it's essential to indulge responsibly:

1. Choose high-quality treats: Look for cat treats from natural ingredients and high-quality protein sources. Avoid treats with artificial additives or excessive fillers.

2. Limit treat intake: Treats should make up no more than 10% of your

cat's daily caloric intake. Overindulging in treats can lead to weight gain and unbalance your cat's diet.

3. Get creative with healthy alternatives: Consider offering your cat healthy treats, like small pieces of cooked, unseasoned meat or fish.

Added thoughts...Some cats are benefited from mixing a small amount of solid-pack pumpkin from a can mixed in their wet food for extra fiber. Also, combing your cat to decrease hair in the intestine and adding pumpkin has helped many constipated cats be more regular.

Many cats get diarrhea from milk. Most adult cats are lactose intolerant.

In conclusion, a healthy, balanced diet is a cornerstone of being the perfect cat owner. By understanding the principles of cat nutrition, learning to decipher food labels, and making informed choices about what to feed your feline friend, you'll be well on your way to ensuring their long-term health and happiness. Bon appétit!

CHAPTER 5
Purrfect Playtime: Building a Strong Bond through Play and Exercise

Playtime is more than just a way to keep your cat and you entertained – it's an essential part of their overall well-being. Cats can exercise their bodies and minds through play, strengthen their bond with you, and indulge their instincts.

The Power of Play: We All Need Play

Cats may be known for being low-maintenance pets, but they still require mental and physical stimulation to stay happy and healthy. Here are just a few reasons why playtime is so essential for your feline friend:

1. Physical health: Regular play sessions help keep your cat's muscles toned, joints flexible, and weight in check. This is particularly important for indoor cats, who may be more prone to obesity and related health issues.

2. Mental stimulation: Cats are intelligent creatures who need mental challenges to prevent boredom and stress. Playtime allows your cat to exercise their problem-solving skills and engage their natural curiosity.

3. Emotional well-being: Playtime can help build a strong bond between you and your cat. A well-bonded cat is more likely to be confident, secure, and affectionate.

4. Instincts: Playtime allows your cat to indulge their natural hunting instincts in a safe and controlled environment.

Choosing the Right Toys: Cat Toys

Just like humans, cats have their preferences when it comes to playthings. Here are some popular types of cat toys to consider for your cat.

1. Interactive toys: These toys encourage your cat to engage in active play with you or on their own. Examples include wand toys, feather teasers, and laser pointers. Be sure to supervise playtime with these toys to prevent accidents, injuries, or eating of the toy. Cats eat their prey, but these toys can cause intestinal obstruction and may require surgical removal. Be careful of strings and threads, which, if swallowed, may require surgery to remove. If you sew...do not leave out the thread, especially with needles attached. Thread, strings, yarn, or even tinsel off the Christmas tree can be swallowed by a cat and cause a linear foreign body obstruction.

2. Puzzle toys: Puzzle toys challenge your cat's mental abilities and

reward them with treats or kibble. These toys can be an excellent way to keep your cat engaged and entertained for hours.

3. Catnip toys: Many cats, but not all, go wild for catnip, a natural herb that stimulates feline senses. Catnip-filled toys, like stuffed mice or kickers, can be great fun for catnip-loving cats. My cat, Taffy, loved catnip. I would toss fresh bits of catnip on the floor, and she loved rolling in it. Unfortunately, catnip loses its freshness, so these toys lose their aromatic charm with time. Some cats get pretty drunk on catnip. Some cats relax with it, and some get so excited that they treat you as prey. Best to take it slow with catnip.

4. Balls and chasers: Cats love to stalk and pounce, and toys that roll or skitter across the floor can be irresistible. Consider adding lightweight balls, crinkle toys, or motorized chasers to your cat's collection. Ping-pong balls and crumbled pieces of paper can be inexpensive and fun for your cat.

However, be alerted to toys they might tear apart and eat or swallow whole.

5. Climbing and scratching toys: Cats love to climb and scratch, so providing appropriate outlets can save your furniture and promote healthy exercise. Cat trees, scratching posts, and wall-mounted shelves are all great options.

Creating Fun and Engaging Play Sessions: Tips for Feline Frolics

Now that you have a treasure trove of toys, it's time to learn how to create engaging play sessions that will delight both you and your cat:

1. Mimic natural hunting behaviors: When playing with your cat, try to replicate the movements and behaviors of their natural prey, like birds or rodents. This will tap into their instincts and make playtime more exciting.

2. Vary the pace and intensity: Like an actual hunt, playtime should have

moments of high energy and excitement and periods of calm and stealth. Vary the speed and intensity of play to keep your cat engaged and interested.

3. Allow your cat to "catch" their prey: During playtime, it's essential to let your cat successfully capture their "prey" occasionally. This helps to build their confidence and provides a sense of satisfaction.

4. Rotate toys to maintain interest: Cats can get bored with the same toys, so try rotating their toy selection to keep things fresh and exciting. For example, put some toys away and reintroduce them later to reignite your cat's interest.

5. Schedule regular play sessions: Aim for two or more play sessions daily, each lasting around 5-10 minutes or until your cat loses interest. Playtime can help prevent boredom and keep your cat's energy levels in check.

6. Encourage solo play: While interactive play sessions are crucial for bonding and mental stimulation, providing opportunities for solo play is essential. For example, scatter some toys around the house or invest in an automatic toy that can entertain your cat when you're not around.

7. Use treats and food puzzles as motivation: Food can be a powerful motivator for cats, so consider incorporating treats or food puzzles into your play sessions. This can be particularly helpful for encouraging play in older or more sedentary cats.

8. Pay attention to your cat's preferences: Every cat is different, and it's essential to observe your cat's play preferences and tailor your play sessions accordingly.

9. Know when to stop: It's crucial to recognize when your cat has had enough playtime and allow them to rest. Overstimulation can lead to stress and aggression, so pay attention to your cat's body language

and end the play session if they show signs of agitation or disinterest.

10. Provide a cool-down period: After an intense play session, it's essential to give your cat a chance to cool down and relax. Offer them a quiet space to rest and consider providing a small treat or meal to help them wind down.

In conclusion, playtime is critical to your cat's overall well-being and essential to being the perfect cat owner. Let the fun begin!

CHAPTER 6
Navigating Health and Wellness: Preventing and Managing Common Feline Health Issues

Being vigilant about your cat's health and wellness is essential as a cat owner. Regular veterinary check-ups, a balanced diet, and a safe environment can help prevent many health issues, but sometimes even the healthiest cats can fall ill. This chapter will discuss some common feline health issues and provide tips on preventing and managing them.

Feline Health Issues: The Most Common Culprits

1. Dental disease: Cats are prone to dental problems like tartar buildup, gingivitis, and stomatitis. Dental disease can lead to tooth loss, infection, and other health issues.

2. Obesity: As indoor pets, cats are at higher risk for obesity, which can lead to joint pain and strain on their hearts.

3. Urinary tract issues: Urinary tract infections, bladder stones, and urinary blockages are common health issues in cats, particularly males. These issues can be painful and even life-threatening if left untreated.

4. Parasites: Fleas, ticks, and worms can cause various cat health problems, including anemia, skin irritation, and disease transmission.

5. Respiratory infections: Upper respiratory infections, or URIs, are viral or bacterial infections that can cause symptoms like sneezing, runny nose, and coughing. These infections are highly contagious and can spread quickly among cats.

Prevention is Key: Tips for Keeping Your Cat Healthy

While not all health issues can be prevented, there are many steps you can take to keep your cat healthy and reduce their risk of developing common health issues:

1. Regular vet check-ups: Annual check-ups with your vet can help detect any health issues early and provide preventive care like vaccinations, parasite prevention, and dental cleanings.

2. A balanced diet: A high-quality diet that meets your cat's nutritional needs can help maintain a healthy weight and prevent obesity. Consult your vet for the appropriate diet for your cat's age, health status, and lifestyle.

3. Exercise and play: Regular exercise can help keep your cat's weight in check and promote overall wellness. Aim for at least 15-20 minutes of playtime daily and provide toys that encourage activity and engagement.

4. Good hygiene: Regular combing and brushing your cat's fur can reduce vomiting up hair. Some cats need to be periodically shaved, especially the longhaired or Persian breeds, during the warmer months to increase their physical comfort, eliminate their matted fur, and decrease the vomiting from hairballs. In addition, some cats need a regular hygienic trim in and around their rear to prevent fecal and urine soiling. Finally, some cats need the tips of their nails trimmed to avoid the nails from growing into their foot pads. Ask your vet for help.

5. Parasite prevention: I recommend a fine-tooth metal flea comb as the first line of detection and defense against fleas. Regular flea and tick preventives and deworming medications may be needed to help keep your cat parasite-free and reduce its risk of related health issues. Indoor cats are less likely to pick up fleas and ticks unless you have dog or cat visitors, or your cat goes outside.

Managing Feline Health Issues: When to Call the Vet

Even with the best preventive care, your cat may still develop health issues. Here are some signs that it's time to call the vet:

1. Changes in appetite or water intake: If your cat suddenly stops eating, drinking, or begins to consume excessive amounts of food or water, it could be a sign of an underlying health issue.

2. Behavioral changes: Changes in your cat's behavior, such as lethargy, hiding, or excessive vocalization, can indicate pain or illness.

3. Respiratory symptoms: Coughing, sneezing, wheezing, or difficulty breathing could indicate a respiratory infection or other health issues.

4. Urinary symptoms: Straining to urinate, blood in the urine, or excessive grooming of the genital

area can be signs of a urinary tract issue.

5. Skin issues: Skin problems like excessive itching, hair loss, or skin lesions can be signs of allergies or other health issues.

6. Vomiting or diarrhea: Occasional vomiting or diarrhea can be normal for cats, but frequent or severe episodes can indicate a digestive or other health problem.

7. Changes in mobility: Difficulty walking, limping, or reluctance to move could indicate joint pain or other issues.

When in doubt, it's always best to consult with your veterinarian. Early intervention can help prevent health issues from becoming more severe and improve your cat's chances of a full recovery.

Tips for Managing Feline Health Issues

If your cat does develop a health issue, there are steps you can take to manage their symptoms and improve their overall well-being:

1. Follow your vet's recommendations: Your vet will provide a treatment plan tailored to your cat's health issue. Follow their recommendations closely, including administering medications as directed and scheduling follow-up appointments.

2. Provide a safe and comfortable environment: Ensure your cat has a quiet and comfortable space to rest and recover. Provide bedding and plenty of water, and keep their litter box clean.

3. Monitor your cat's symptoms: Keep a close eye on your cat's symptoms and report any changes or concerns to your vet. Record details like appetite, water intake, and

behavior to give your vet a complete picture of your cat's health.

4. Adjust their diet: Depending on the health issue, your cat's diet may need to be adjusted. For example, your vet may recommend a special diet or specific feeding schedule to manage your cat's symptoms.

5. Provide emotional support: Cats can become stressed or anxious when unwell. Offer your cat plenty of affection and reassurance. Distraction and play, for some cats, can be helpful. A quiet place to rest and hide may be the least stressful. Some cats appreciate a box to curl up and hide in.

In conclusion, navigating feline health and wellness can be challenging, but with proper preventive care and early intervention, you can help your cat stay healthy and happy. By understanding common health issues, following your vet's recommendations, and providing a safe and supportive environment, you'll be well-equipped to handle health issues that may arise. Remember, your cat's health and well-being are in your hands – so take good care of your feline friend!

CHAPTER 7
Feline Socialization: Building Strong Relationships with Other Cats and Humans

Cats are often considered solitary but social animals that can benefit from positive relationships with other cats and humans. In this chapter, we'll explore the world of feline socialization and provide tips on how to help your cat build strong relationships.

The Importance of Feline Socialization

Socialization is how cats learn to interact and communicate with others, including cats and humans. Positive socialization experiences can help your cat feel confident, secure, and happy. Here are some of the benefits of socialization:

1. Improved health: Socialized cats may be less likely to develop stress-related health issues like digestive problems or respiratory infections.

2. Reduced aggression: Cats with positive socialization experiences are less likely to behave aggressively towards other cats or humans.

3. Better mental and emotional well-being: Socialized cats tend to be more confident, curious, and outgoing, which can improve their overall mental and emotional health.

4. Enhanced human-cat bond: Socialized cats tend to have stronger bonds with their human companions, which can improve the quality of the human-cat relationship.

Socializing Your Cat with Other Cats

If you have more than one cat or plan to introduce a new one to your household, providing opportunities for positive socialization is essential. Here are some tips for introducing your cat to other cats:

1. Take it slow: Introductions should be done slowly and carefully, allowing each cat to adjust to the presence of the other. Start with scent swapping – allow each cat to sniff the other's bedding or toys – before progressing to visual and physical introductions.

2. Use positive reinforcement: Reward positive behavior with treats, praise, or playtime. Encourage your cats to interact positively, such as playing or grooming each other.

3. Provide separate resources: Cats can become territorial over food, water, and litter boxes. Provide separate resources for each cat to prevent conflict.

4. Supervise interactions: Initially, it's essential to supervise any interactions between your cats. If you notice signs of aggression or

stress, separate the cats and try again later.

5. Be patient: The socialization process can take time, and each cat will progress at their own pace. So be patient, and don't rush the process.

Socializing Your Cat with Humans

Here are some tips for socializing your cat with humans:

1. Start early: Kittens exposed to positive human interaction at an early age are more likely to become friendly and outgoing cats.

2. Use positive reinforcement: Reward positive behavior with treats, praise, or playtime. Encourage your cat to interact with humans in a positive way, such as sitting on laps or playing.

3. Respect your cat's boundaries: Cats have their preferences regarding touch and interaction. Respect your cat's boundaries; don't

force interactions if they're uninterested.

4. Provide opportunities for play and exploration: Playtime and exploration can help your cat feel confident and comfortable around humans. Provide toys, scratching posts, and other activities to encourage your cat to engage with you.

5. Be patient: Socialization can take time, especially with older cats that may be more set in their ways.

In conclusion, socialization is a crucial aspect of feline care and companionship. By providing opportunities for positive interactions with other cats and humans, you can help your cat build solid relationships and lead a happy and healthy life.

Remember to take things slow, use positive reinforcement, and be patient with your cat's progress. With the right approach and plenty of love and attention, your cat will thrive and become a cherished companion for years.

Feline socialization can be challenging, but the benefits are worth the effort. Not only can socialization improve your cat's physical and mental well-being, but it can also enhance your relationship with your feline friend. With the tips and strategies in this chapter, you'll be well on your way to building a solid bond with your cat and ensuring their long-term happiness and well-being.

In addition to socialization, there are many other aspects of feline care and companionship to consider. By mastering the art of feline care, you can provide your cat with everything they need to lead a healthy, happy life.

From nutrition and exercise to playtime and socialization, every aspect of care plays a role in your cat's overall well-being. By understanding your cat's unique needs and preferences and tailoring your care approach accordingly, you can become the perfect cat owner and provide your feline friend with a lifetime of love and companionship.

CHAPTER 8
Safety First

Creating a Safe and Stimulating Environment: Ensuring Your Cat's Physical and Mental Well-being

Creating a safe and stimulating environment that meets your cat's physical and mental needs is essential for a cat owner. In this chapter, we'll explore the critical elements of a cat-friendly environment and provide tips on creating the perfect space for your feline friend.

Designing a Safe and Secure Environment

Safety should be a top priority when creating your cat's living space. Here are some tips to ensure a safe and secure environment:

1. Choose cat-friendly materials: Avoid materials that can be toxic or dangerous to cats, such as certain plants or chemicals. Opt for safe materials like non-toxic cleaning supplies and plants for cats. Toxic plants are of concern. Lilies top the list of flowers not to have in your house. Don't buy or give lilies to anyone who might have a cat. If your cat can enter your garage, ensure they don't lap up any spilled antifreeze.

Go to www.PetPoisonHelpline.com for a list of toxins to avoid.

2. Secure windows and doors: Cats are curious creatures that love to explore. Ensure your windows and doors are secure to prevent your cat from escaping or falling from a high surface.

3. Provide a safe space: Cats need a safe and comfortable space to retreat when stressed or overwhelmed. Provide a cozy cat bed or a hiding

spot like a cardboard box or cat tunnel. Some people create an enclosed outdoor play area for their cats called a catio.

4. Eliminate hazards: Eliminate hazards like loose cords or dangling blinds that can harm your cat. Keep electrical cords out of reach or cover them with cord protectors. Christmas trees with dangling ornaments, tinsel, and strings of lights can be hard for some cats to resist.

5. Provide scratching surfaces: Cats must scratch to maintain healthy claws and relieve stress. Provide scratching posts or surfaces appropriate for your cat's size and preference.

Creating a Stimulating and Enriching Environment

In addition to safety, your cat's living space should provide plenty of opportunities for stimulation and enrichment. Here are some tips to ensure a stimulating and enriching environment:

1. Provide toys and time to play with your cat: Toys can help your cat stay active and engaged. Provide a variety of toys like balls, feather wands, or puzzle feeders to keep your cat and you entertained. Consider getting another cat or even a dog as a playmate companion. One of my cat's favorite toys is called the Cat Dancer. On YouTube...there is a video ...called Cat Dancer Original Cat Teaser on a Wire Interactive Cat Toy. I like to watch episodes of Animal Planet's My Cat From Hell. I don't always agree with how Jackson Galaxy sometimes pushes the situation beyond what I would consider safe. People can get hurt, and so can cats. If you ever go to rescue an injured or upset cat...wait

for someone adequately trained to help if you can. A thick blanket or a thick towel is what we sometimes use in the clinic to wrap a cat. Your injured or hurt pet may bite or scratch out of fear and pain. I always carry a pair of fireplace gloves, a towel, a blanket, and a carrier in the trunk of my car for emergencies.

2. Offer perches and climbing opportunities: Cats love to climb and explore their surroundings. Provide perches or climbing structures like cat trees or shelves to allow your cat to explore their space vertically.

3. Provide access to windows: Cats love to watch the world go by from a comfortable perch. Provide access to windows with a view and consider adding a bird feeder or squirrel feeder outside to keep your cat entertained. Some cats can be stressed by things that they see or hear outside. Watch your cat...if signs of upset occur, there may be a stray cat outside that needs to be blocked from your cat's view and out of hearing range.

4. Play with your cat: Interactive playtime can help strengthen the bond between you and your cat. Set aside time each day to play with your cat using toys like feather wands or maybe the Cat Dancer, my cat's favorite. Itty was adopted from the shelter, and I adopted a second cat, Mellie, who was a great match. Some cats at the shelter are already bonded to another cat, and it is a great opportunity and an act of generosity and kindness to adopt the pair together.

5. Provide a variety of textures: Cats love to explore different textures; provide a variety of textures like soft blankets, plush toys, and scratchy surfaces to keep your cat engaged.

Improving Your Cat's Quality of Life

Creating a safe and stimulating environment can help improve your cat's quality of life in many ways. Here are some of the benefits of a cat-friendly environment:

1. Reduced stress: A comfortable and safe environment can help reduce stress and anxiety in cats, improving their overall well-being. Petting your cat can be mutually beneficial. It can lower your blood pressure, and the cat that loves it will melt into it or even request it.

2. Enhanced physical health: A stimulating environment that encourages play and exercise can improve your cat's physical health and prevent obesity and related health issues.

3. Improved mental and emotional well-being: A stimulating and enriching environment can improve your cat's mental and emotional well-being, leading to a happier and healthier cat.

4. Enhanced human-cat bond: Providing a safe and stimulating environment can also strengthen the bond between you and your cat, improving the quality of your relationship.

In conclusion, creating a safe and stimulating environment is essential for ensuring your cat's physical and mental well-being. By providing safe and comfortable living space, offering plenty of toys and activities, and spending quality time with your cat, you can help your feline friend lead a happy and healthy life.

Remember, every cat is unique, and what works for one cat may not work for another. Take the time to understand your cat's preferences and needs, and tailor their environment accordingly. With creativity and attention to detail, you can create the perfect setting for your feline friend and ensure their long-term well-being.

In addition to creating a safe and stimulating environment, there are many other aspects of feline care and companionship to consider. By mastering the art of feline care, you can provide your cat with everything they need to lead a healthy, happy life. From nutrition and exercise to playtime and socialization, every aspect of care plays a role in your cat's overall well-being. By understanding your cat's unique needs and preferences and tailoring your care approach accordingly, you can become the perfect cat parent and provide your feline friend with a lifetime of love and companionship.

CHAPTER 9
Traveling with Your Cat: Tips for a Safer Trip

Traveling in a car for many cats isn't fun for them, or you, and it is best to plan if possible.

Preparing for Your Trip

1. Going to the vet: Your vet may also recommend medication or other strategies to help your cat stay calm during the trip.

2. Some cats are better served with a house call visit by the veterinarian. For example, some cats hide when visitors come, and it may be best to have them in their carriers or in a room like a bathroom where there are no beds to dash under and hide come exam time.

3. Invest in a secure carrier: A safe and comfortable carrier is essential for your cat's safety and well-being during travel. Choose an appropriately sized carrier for your cat that provides adequate ventilation and visibility.

4. Temperature concerns: Interiors of cars can get very hot on sunny days. Don't leave your cat alone in the car. A shaded area with the air conditioner running can make it more comfortable and safer for you and your cat.

5. Familiarize your cat with the carrier: Help your cat get accustomed to it before the trip by leaving it open in a comfortable space and encouraging your cat to explore it. Consider placing treats or favorite toys in the carrier to make it a positive and inviting space. Next, take the cat in the carrier to the car, and you two sit together. Open the carrier slightly to give your cat some affection, and once they start purring or at least more relaxed, you can go back into the house, having rewarded

your kitty for being calm in a carrier in the car.

Traveling with Your Cat

Once you've prepared for the trip. Here are some tips for traveling with your cat:

1. Keep your cat secure: During travel, it's essential to keep your cat in the carrier to prevent injury or escape. Also, avoid letting your cat roam freely in the car, and never allow your cat to ride on your lap while driving.

2. For short trips: No food or water and fasting may be required or requested by your veterinarian for specific blood tests and procedures.

3. Keep your cat calm: Travel can be stressful for cats, so taking steps to keep your cat calm and comfortable is essential. Consider using a calming pheromone spray or medication recommended by your veterinarian.

4. For longer trips: Provide opportunities for food, water, a chance to use the litter box, and to stretch their legs. Wait to open the car door until the cat is secured. If you are in a motel, don't open the door until your cat is secured. Cats can be trained to a harness or need to be in their carriers or closed in the bathroom when someone comes in and out of your motel or hotel room. Put up the "do not disturb sign" and decline maid service. It is not worth losing your cat in a strange city if they slip through an open door or window.

5. Provide affection and reassurance: During travel, your cat may need extra affection and reassurance to feel secure. Offer attention and praise and provide a favorite toy or blanket to help your cat feel comfortable.

In conclusion, traveling with your cat is sometimes necessary, and it is best to be prepared to make it safe and stress-free as possible for everyone.

CHAPTER 10
Senior Cat Care: Tips for Supporting Your Aging Feline Friend

As cats age, their needs and preferences can change, requiring adjustments to their care routine. As a cat owner, you must provide your aging feline friend with the support and care they need to enjoy their golden years. This chapter will explore tips and strategies for senior cat care and how to ensure your aging cat's well-being.

Understanding Your Senior Cat's Needs

As cats age, they may experience changes in their physical and cognitive abilities. Here are some common changes that occur in senior cats:

1. Decreased mobility: Senior cats may experience decreased mobility, making it more challenging for them to climb, jump, or access their litter box.

2. Changes in appetite: Senior cats may experience changes in appetite, either eating less or becoming more selective about their food. Some cats develop ravenous appetites and lose weight due to an overactive thyroid. Some cats start drinking more water and urinating more than before.

3. Dental problems: Senior cats are more susceptible to dental issues, affecting their overall health.

4. Cognitive decline: Senior cats may experience cognitive decline, including changes in their sleep-wake cycle, confusion, and memory problems.

5. Changes in behavior: Senior cats may exhibit changes in behavior, such as increased vocalization or aggression, which can indicate underlying health issues.

Tips for Senior Cat Care

Adjusting their care routine to meet their changing needs is essential to ensure your senior cat's well-being. Here are some tips for senior cat care:

1. Visit your vet regularly: Senior cats should visit the veterinarian at least twice a year for a checkup and to address any health concerns. In addition, your vet may recommend additional tests or treatments to ensure your cat's well-being.

2. Provide a comfortable living space: Senior cats may benefit from a comfortable and secure living space that meets their changing physical and cognitive abilities. Consider providing a cozy bed or a litter box with low sides to accommodate mobility challenges. Consider putting a night light near the litter box and an extra cat box downstairs or upstairs if they have multiple stories and stairs to climb. Provide additional water bowls with fresh water in various locations.

3. Adjust their diet: Senior cats may require a special diet to meet their changing nutritional needs. Consult your veterinarian to determine the best diet for your aging feline friend.

4. Provide dental care: Senior cats are more susceptible to dental problems, so it's essential to provide regular dental care.

5. Encourage exercise: Senior cats still need exercise, but their mobility may be limited. Provide low-impact activities like gentle play or short walks to keep your cat active and healthy.

6. Monitor changes in behavior: Senior cats may exhibit changes in behavior that can indicate underlying health issues. For example, watch for changes in appetite, behavior, or mobility, and consult with your veterinarian if you notice anything unusual.

7. Provide affection and attention: Senior cats may need extra attention and affection to feel comfortable and

secure. Spend time with your cat, provide plenty of affection, and offer a comfortable and safe space for them to relax and rest.

In conclusion, providing senior cat care requires attention and adjustment to meet your aging feline friend's changing needs. By consulting with your veterinarian, adjusting its diet and living space, providing dental care, encouraging exercise or movement, monitoring changes in behavior, and offering affection and attention, you can support your senior cat's well-being and help them enjoy their golden years. With these tips and strategies, you can become the perfect cat parent and provide your feline friend with a lifetime of love, care, and companionship, even in their senior years.

ABOUT THE AUTHOR

Dr. Garrett graduated with her Doctor of Veterinary Medicine degree from the University of California at Davis in 1976 and has spent decades in a veterinary practice devoted to cats.

Dr. Garrett is working on a new book supporting nonprofits, including the local animal shelter where she adopted her cat Itty.

She is dedicated to making a positive difference in the lives of animals and those who love them.

It all started at seven when she fell in love with a kitten named Angel.

www.PuttingLove1st.com

Made in the USA
Las Vegas, NV
04 June 2024